JUST LOOK AT...

WATER
TRAVEL

JUST LOOK AT...
WATER TRAVEL

Bill Gunston

Rourke Enterprises, Inc.
Vero Beach, FL 32964

Distributed by Marshall Cavendish

Factual adviser: Aubrey Tulley

Editor: Stephen White-Thomson
Teacher Panel: John Allen, Tim Firth,
Lynne McCoombe
Designer: Ewing Paddock
Production: Rosemary Bishop
Picture Research: Diana Morris

Illustrations
Peter Dennis/Linda Rogers Associates 26
Keith Duran/Linden Artists 25, 29
Tony Gibbons/Linden Artists 16–17, 18–19,
32–33, 40–41
Keith Maddison Cover cartoon, 8, 12, 22, 24
Janos Marffy/Jillian Burgess 10–11, 14, 20, 23,
36–37
Clifford Meadway 43

Photographs
Aldus Archive: 30T.
BBC Hulton Picture Library: 31T.
Cosmos: 27B © Don King.
Robert Harding: 34.
Michael Holford: 22T.
Hutchison Library: title page, 9BL, 37.
Pickthall Picture Library: 39B, 40.
Planet Earth/Seaphot: 19.
Derek Pratt: 36.
Rex: 41.
RNLI: 10.
Science Museum: 30B.
Science Photo Library: 22B.
Ronald Sheridan: 28B.
Tony Stone: 15, 34–35.
TASS: 33T.
Zefa: cover, 9T, 9BR, 13T, 13B, 16, 21T, 21B, 25,
27T, 28T, 31B, 33B, 39TL, 39TR.

Title page photo: Boating on a lake in Kashmir,
India

Library of Congress Cataloging in Publication Data

Gunston, Bill.
  Water travel.

  (Just look at . . .)
  Includes index.
  Summary: Examines how boats and ships have
transported people and cargo through the ages and
how they are designed and used today.
  1. Boats and boating—Juvenile literature.
2. Ships—Juvenile literature.   3. Navigation—
Juvenile literature.   [1. Boats and boating.
2. Ships]   I. Title.   II. Series.
VM150.G86 1987   623.8   87-16415
ISBN 0-86592-992-0

How to use this book
Look first in the contents page to see if the subject you want is listed. For instance, if you want to find out about racing on water you will find the information on pages 38 and 39. The word list explains the more difficult terms found in this book. The index will tell you how many times a particular subject is mentioned and whether there is a picture of it.

Water Travel is one of a series of books on Transport. All books on this subject have a purple color band around the cover. If you want to know more about transport, look for other books with a purple band in the **Just Look At. . .** series.

© 1987 Rourke Enterprises, Inc.
© 1987 Macdonald & Co. (Publishers) Ltd.

CONTENTS

ON TO WATER

All over the world people use vehicles to move from one place to another. We use vehicles to mean not just cars and buses but airplanes, ships and every other kind of invention for carrying things and people. Some vehicles were invented less than 100 years ago, but the oldest vehicle of all is the boat.

We cannot say exactly when the first boat was made, but we know that it was many thousands of years ago. People in different parts of the world invented different kinds of boat. Some were simple canoes, hollowed out of tree trunks. Some were rafts made of special light logs tied together. Some were made from reeds and long grasses tightly woven and made watertight. Others were light wooden frames with stretched animal skins over them. They were used to travel short distances, mostly on lakes and rivers.

About 5,000 years ago the people of the Middle East were building ships which could travel across the sea. Since then, people have used ships to explore the Earth. Today, ships are made of many different materials, in many sizes and shapes. Some have sails or paddles, but most have engines. Some are for carrying goods or people, some are for fun, some for racing, some for fighting and some for exploring deep below the sea.

On the right, is a canoe in Kashmir, India. It is so heavily laden it seems to be on the point of sinking! ▶

On the far right, this Indian bulk carrier is like hundreds of other modern ships that carry the world's trade. It is almost empty; when full of cargo, the red part of the hull is under water.

◀ Playing with model boats is a popular hobby for many children.

The fastest form of water travel for ordinary passengers is the hovercraft which rides along on a cushion of air. This SR.N4 'flies' between England and France. It carries 60 cars and 416 passengers at speeds of up to 75 mph.

Dover·Ramsgate·Calais·Boulogne

HOVERSPEED

PARVATI

Staying Afloat

Have you tried to hold a table tennis ball under water? As you push the ball down, you can feel the water pushing against it. Let go and the ball shoots up to float on the surface. That force pushing the ball up is called upthrust.

Likewise, a floating boat or ship is supported by the upthrust of the surrounding water. For a vessel to float, this upward force must equal the total weight of the vessel, including anything it is carrying.

As a ship is loaded with cargo or passengers, it sinks deeper into the water. It sinks until the amount of water it pushes aside balances the total weight of ship and cargo.

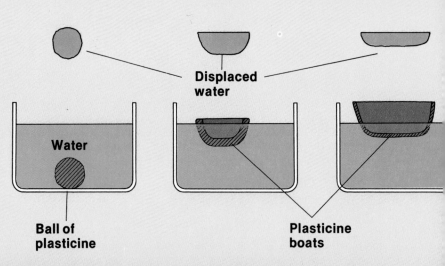

Rod

Pivot

Thread

▲ These two balls of plasticine are the same. They balance each other.

Water

▲ If one is immersed in water it appears to weigh much less.

Here we have a ball of plasticine. If we place it in water it displaces a ball of water. This weighs slightly less than the plasticine does and the plasticine ball sinks. To make plasticine float in water we must make it hollow. ▼

If we mould the plasticine into the shape of a crude boat with very thick sides and bottom, we can make the plasticine float. It sinks into the water until the boat-shaped displaced water weighs the same as the plasticine does. ▼

If we make our boat big by making its sides and bottom thinner, then it floats much higher in the water, displacing a large but shallow volume of water. This is why a ship can be made of metal and still float. ▼

Displaced water

Water

Ball of plasticine

Plasticine boats

Lifeboats are launched as fast as possible by sliding down a skipway leading from their shed to the sea. They have to be buoyant enough to stay afloat in the roughest sea.

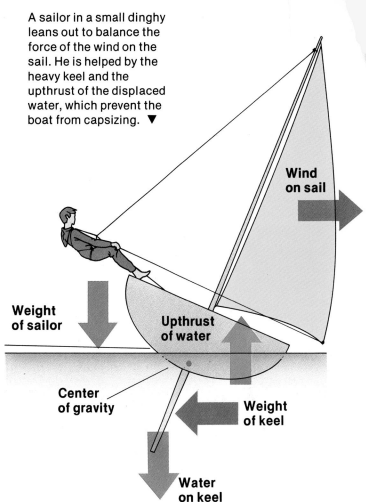

A sailor in a small dinghy leans out to balance the force of the wind on the sail. He is helped by the heavy keel and the upthrust of the displaced water, which prevent the boat from capsizing. ▼

Wind on sail

Weight of sailor

Upthrust of water

Center of gravity

Weight of keel

Water on keel

...lacement

...unloaded ship weighs 40,000 tons, then it ...t push aside 40,000 tons of water. If a ship is ...ed with 1,000 tons of cargo then it sinks until ...xtra 1,000 tons of water is displaced (41,000 ... in all). The weight of a ship is called its ...lacement. It displaces that amount of water.

...ing

...maged ship will sink completely if the weight ...e ship and its cargo *plus* the weight of the ...r getting in, eventually become greater than ...veight of the water pushed aside by the ...ng ship.

...soll lines

...n a ship is in fresh river water it sinks a little ...er than it would in sea water. This is because ...bic centimeter of fresh water weighs slightly ...than a cubic centimeter of sea water. So, ...fresh water has to be pushed aside to ...ort the ship.

A ship cannot safely carry as much cargo in fresh water as in salt water. Fresh water and sea water marks — Plimsoll lines — are painted on the side of a ship to show safe loading levels.

Capsizing

If a boat rolls over and turns upside down we say it has capsized. Small sailing dinghies quite often capsize, but they do not sink and usually can be pulled upright again, but if a big ship were to capsize it would be terrible. Probably it would sink. Look at the diagram to see what forces are acting on the dinghy. If certain forces are stronger than other forces, the dinghy will capsize.

Lifeboats are special boats that rescue people in danger on the sea. They have to stay afloat in very bad weather. Modern lifeboats are designed so that they can capsize and then turn right way up again, without anybody helping.

Muscle Power

The first boats had nothing to make them go along. They just floated along rivers, carried by the current. To go upstream, against the current, or to cross a lake, people had to invent a way of making the boat go forward.

The simplest method was to paddle with the hands. When you push against something it pushes back against you. The forces are equal and act in opposite directions. If you pull the water backwards, the water will pull you forwards. This is what happens when you swim.

Paddles

People soon learned that you could paddle a boat better if you held something large and flat, bigger than your hand. The first paddles were probably flat pieces of wood. Gradually people learned how to make one end into a paddle and the other end into a handle. If you keep paddling on the same side of the boat you will find the boat usually goes in a curve. To go in a straight line you have to paddle first on the left and then on the right. Soon people began using double-ended paddles, so that one person could easily paddle rather in the way we walk: left, right, left, right. . .

Oars

Thousands of years ago it was discovered that the boat will go faster if you make the paddle very long. This works better if you make a pivot for the paddle on the side of the boat. About 500 BC Greeks and Phoenicians (people who lived in what is now Lebanon) started to build ships, called galleys, which were propelled by lots of long paddles, called oars. The rowers were usually slaves. They worked very hard.

This American Indian is paddling his canoe. He is about to dip the paddle into the water. ▼

Here he has dipped the wide part of the paddle in and is pulling it back through the water. ▼

Then he lifts it out so that he only pushes air out of the way as he brings it forward again. ▼

▲ Coxed fours (four rowers plus a cox to steer) are racing hard. Notice the places in the water where the oars just came out.

Rowing races

Today, boats using oars and paddles are used mostly for sport and leisure. The fastest boats ever propelled by muscle power are today's 'racing eights'. They are rowed by eight people who are chosen because of their strength, fitness and skill with an oar. They are very long, thin boats. The oars are pivoted a long way out from the side of the boat. As the rower pulls back on the handle of the oar he pulls the blade of the oar through the water which pushes the boat forward.

Different kinds of rowing

In some parts of the world people put the oar the other way around and push it! This lets them see where they are going instead of where they have been. Some oarsmen stand at the back and propel the boat by working a single oar from side to side in various ways. Some of the slave galleys worked their oars like this, swinging the oars in and out, instead of to front and rear. On some British rivers, people propel boats, called punts, by pushing against the bottom of the river with a long pole.

Huge canoes race in Hong Kong's Dragon Boat Festival. Each canoe is paddled by about 40 strong men. ▼

Wind Power

Paddling a boat is hard work, so people long ago searched for other methods of propelling a boat forward. They learned to harness the power of the wind to move their boats. Sails were needed to 'catch' the wind. They made sails from large areas of material and fastened them to pieces of wood that crossed an upright pole called the mast. Sailors soon learned that they could catch more of the wind and make the boat go faster by pulling on ropes connected to the sail's bottom corners.

Forces on sails

Though the pressure of the wind is small, sails can be so large that the force on the whole area can be measured in tons! If the wind gets too strong, it can rip sails clean off the ship. Sailors had to learn when a storm was coming.

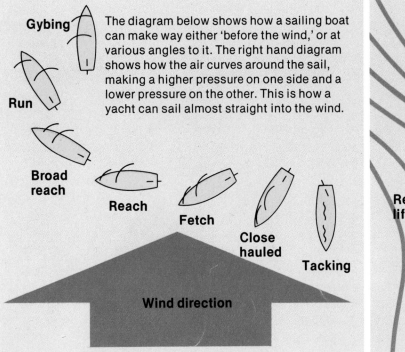

The diagram below shows how a sailing boat can make way either 'before the wind,' or at various angles to it. The right hand diagram shows how the air curves around the sail, making a higher pressure on one side and a lower pressure on the other. This is how a yacht can sail almost straight into the wind.

Gybing

Run

Broad reach

Reach

Fetch

Close hauled

Tacking

Wind direction

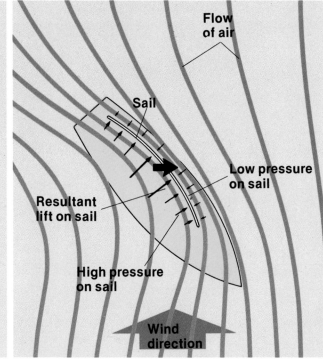

Flow of air

Sail

Low pressure on sail

Resultant lift on sail

High pressure on sail

Wind direction

The wind in these colorful sails make the racing yachts travel very fast.

Then they would take down and roll up the sails. Changing the sails was difficult and dangerous work that had to be done in all weathers.

As ships got bigger they were fitted with more sails, fixed to taller masts. The forces on the sails push the ship along but also try to roll it over, or make it tilt so that the front (the bow) goes down and the back (the stern comes up. Small sailing boats are often blown almost flat, with the crew leaning out to balance the force of the wind.

Against the wind
Different arrangements of sails are called rigs. It took thousands of years for sailors to improve on the old kind of sail, called square-rigged, which is blown along by a wind blowing from behind. About 1,200 years ago Arab sailors fixed a sail in what was called the lateen rig.

The sail was almost in line with the hull. Arabs found that by pulling on ropes and curving the sail they could make the boat go forward with the wind blowing from the side.

Improved rigs allowed sailors to do a maneuver called tacking. By first swinging the sail to the left (sailors call this direction port) and then to the right (starboard) they could make their boat travel in a zig-zag. Each bit of the journey had the wind just enough from the side for the sail to push the boat along.

The rigs of today's racing yachts are so well designed that they can sail almost directly into the wind. Look at the diagram to see how a sail acts like a wing on water. The yacht heads into the wind which blows against the sail. The pressure on one side of the sail is greater than on the other so that the resulting force on the sail drives the boat forwards.

15

Engine Power

For hundreds of years inventors tried to think of ways to propel a ship with an engine. Unlike a slave's muscles, engines do not get tired, but can work at full power as long as they are supplied with fuel. But first, an engine had to be designed. Then a way had to be found to make it drive a ship along.

Steam power

The first practical engine was the steam engine. Water is boiled in a container called a boiler. The pressure in the boiler increases.

The only way the steam can get out is through a pipe leading to a cylinder. This cylinder contains a piston which can slide up and down inside the cylinder. Steam is fed to one side of the piston, pushing it along the cylinder. Then the steam is fed to the other side of the piston, pushing it the other way.

The piston is connected to a rod, with a pivot at each end, and the up-and-down motion of the rod is turned into the around-and-around motion of a long shaft by something called a crank. In the first steamships the shaft was connected to large paddlewheels. Flat paddles fixed around the wheels acted like revolving oars.

The propeller

Later the shaft was connected to a propeller. Propellers are sometimes called 'screws', because they move through the water like a screw going into a piece of wood. They have twisted blades which fan outwards from a central point. As the propeller goes around, the blades push the water backwards and the ship is driven forward.

Steam turbines

At the end of the 1800s, Sir Charles Parsons made the first useful steam turbine. Instead of driving a piston up and down a cylinder, the steam is piped to a box containing a turbine rotor. This is a shaft carrying hundreds of blades like small windmill blades. The steam rushes past these blades, like wind past a windmill, and turns the shaft. Turbines turn much faster than piston-type engines, so quite small turbines can be very powerful.

◀ Workers in this shipyard have just fixed the propeller on a new ship. Behind the propeller is the huge rudder, for steering.

▲ The *Great Eastern* was far bigger than any other ship in 1858 whan it was launched. It had sails, and engines to drive propellers and paddle wheels. The engine on the right drove the *Great Eastern's* paddle wheels.

Paddlewheel

Crankshaft

Crank

Crankshaft

Piston (inside a cylinder)

Steam pipe

Crank

Boiler

Paddlewheel

Furnace

Cylinders

Cylinder

Piston rods

The first turbine boat, *Turbinia*, reached over 40 mph in 1897, twice as fast as any other boat. Steam turbines are still used in some big ships, and in all nuclear-powered ships. In nuclear-powered ships the heat of a nuclear reactor turns the water to steam.

Diesel engines
Small pleasure boats often have gas engines like cars. Most larger ships have diesel engines.

These diesel engines burn oil, and are cheap to run. Very fast boats, such as hydrofoils and hovercraft, sometimes have gas-turbine engines. But diesels are cheaper to buy, so nearly all the latest hydrofoils and hovercraft are driven by diesel engines. Some diesel engines drive air propellers. Others drive water jets. The engine drives a pump which sucks up water and squirts it out at the back, powering the boat along.

Under the Water

This submarine can fire missiles from giant tubes. One tube has been cut away to show the missle inside. It can also fire torpedoes (anti-ship missiles) from tubes in the bow. At the stern is the nuclear steam turbine driving the propeller. Many of the crew work computers and other electronics.

For hundreds of years people have wanted to explore under the sea. But it was not until 1690 that the famous astronomer Halley invented the first successful diving bell which allowed people to breath air below the water's surface. If you put a clear tumbler upside down into water, the air will be trapped inside it. Halley's Bell worked in the same way.

Missile hatches

Missle

Steam turbine

Propeller

Propeller shaft

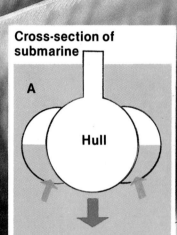

Cross-section of submarine

A

Hull

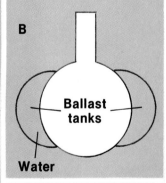

B

Ballast tanks

Water

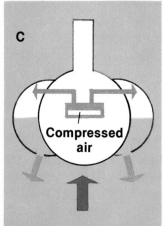

C

Compressed air

Submarines

Submarines are boats that can dive into the sea and then return to the surface. The first practical submarines were made around the year 1900. They were small, cramped and dangerous. They went very slowly, and the air inside quickly grew hot and unfit to breath.

Diving and surfacing

Modern submarines have a strong hull shaped like a cigar. Before diving, the crew check that every door in the submarine is tightly closed. Then valves (large taps) are opened, letting the sea flood special tanks called ballast tanks inside the submarine. As the water comes in, the submarine sinks lower in the water and eventually disappears below the surface.

When a submarine wants to dive (diagram A) sea water is let in (blue arrows) to fill tanks surrounding the main hull. The submarine starts to go down (red arrow). When it is at its maximum depth under the surface (B) the submarine has its ballast tanks full of water. To return to the surface (C) compressed air is pumped under tremendous pressure (orange pipes) to blow out the sea water (blue arrows). The submarine rise (red arrow). ▶

Air
vent
Radar

Periscope

Main
control room

Sonar
detector

Torpedo
tubes

The Perry Cubmarine is a
useful little submersible
vehicle used by a company
called International
Underwater Contractors.
People get in through the
big round doors on top and
can look out through the
portholes in the strong
watertight body. ▶

Ballast
tank

To surface, very highly compressed air is let
into the ballast tanks (see diagram). This blows
out the water and the submarine rises. Modern
submarines have control surfaces like small
wings which help them dive and climb.

Power under water

Until 1960 nearly all submarines had diesel
engines. These needed lots of air, which had to
be sucked in by a pipe sticking out of the sea.
Another pipe got rid of the exhaust. Today many
submarines have nuclear-powered engines. They
can travel faster, dive deeper and stay down two
years! The crew of today's submarines have every
modern comfort. They breath fresh, recycled air
and sea water is drawn in and turned into fresh
water for drinking and washing.

The deepest divers

Submarines that dive to the deepest parts of the
ocean are called submersibles. In some parts of
the ocean, the sea floor is 7 miles from the
surface. The crushing pressure at such a depth is
545 lbs. per centimeter, or about the weight of four
cars on an area the size of a postage stamp!

Submersibles are used by scientists to explore
the ocean and study what they find. Some
divers live under water for weeks aboard
submersibles. Underwater explorer, Jacques
Cousteau, studied plants and animals on the
sea-bed in the submersible Alvin. Submersibles
are small enough to be carried aboard a support
ship and lowered into the sea where they are
needed.

'Flying' on Water

Most ships and boats are slow, compared with cars and trains. This is because the hull, which goes deep into the water, is always having to push the water out of the way.

For more than 150 years people have tried to invent a way of travelling over the water without having a deeply submerged hull. If only a boat could somehow slide on top of the water it could go much faster.

Hydrofoils
The first successful answer to the problem was the hydrofoil. A hydrofoil is a wing that works not in the air but in water. Enrico Forlanini of Italy built the first successful hydrofoil. It reached a speed of 40 mph in 1906.

Ladder foils
The first hydrofoil boats used ladder foils. At rest the boat floats deep in the water in the usual way. Under it are fixed what look like ladders, but the rungs are thin hydrofoils.

As the boat moves forward these push upward, lifting the hull a little. As the hull rises, it pushes less water out of the way and the speed increases. Higher speed means more lift from the foils, lifting the boat higher. At full speed the hull is out of the water, and the weight is supported by just the bottom few hydrofoils.

Surface-piercing foils
Another type of foil is the surface-piercing foil. The boat has just two big foils which slope upwards on each side. As the speed increases, the outer parts of the foil come out of the water. At full speed the hull 'flies' over the sea, supported by just the lowest, central part of each foil.

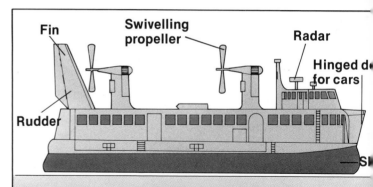

This hovercraft carries passengers and cars. It is driven along by air propellers and lifted by a cushion of air (red arrows below).

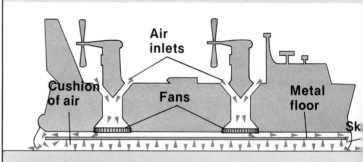

The air is sucked in from above and compressed by large fans. It flows over a metal floor and fills the rubberized, flexible 'skirt'.

Deep foils
Some of the newest hydrofoil boats ride on three tall vertical struts supported on small foils deep in the sea. These deep foils cut through the water underneath all the waves. Some have control systems, like aircraft, to adjust the angle of the foils and keep the boat running smoothly and fast in a rough sea.

Air cushions
In 1959 Sir Christopher Cockerell's ACV (Air-Cushion Vehicle), popularly called a hovercraft, made its first successful 'flight.' The hovercraft moved about on land or water, supported by a cushion of air at a pressure just a little higher than that of the atmosphere.

Engines drive big fans which keep blowing air into the air cushion. By adding a flexible rubber 'skirt' round the outside of the metal 'floor,' the air cushion can be made much deeper, to help the vehicle ride at high speed over waves or rough ground.

In 1966 passengers were ferried across the English Channel by a hovercraft for the first time. Since then, hovercraft have made regular Channel crossings.

▲ A surfer surfs across the rising part of a giant wave. Surfing is an exciting and popular sport.

The central part of the foil lifts the hull of this passenger-carrying hydrofoil above the waves. ▼

Finding your way

The first travellers on water went down rivers or across lakes, so they could not get completely lost. But imagine you are a sailor leaving port and heading straight out to sea. How would you navigate out of sight of land?

Early navigation

Before the 1400s, maps were hopelessly inaccurate and nautical instruments were primitive. During the 1400s ship design improved and so did the quality of instruments to help sailors navigate. On longer voyages into the unknown, explorers carried a magnetic compass which told them the direction to the north magnetic pole. They measured their speed by throwing one end of a knotted string overboard. They could tell their speed by counting how many evenly spaced knots on the string were unrolled in a certain time, measured by a sand-glass.

▲ 500 years ago sailors navigated using a cross-staff. They looked through two sets of holes at the Sun and at the horizon, sliding the cross-piece until the holes lined up.

The user of this sextant rotates an arms with mirrors until two images of the Sun or a star come together. The angle of the arm then gives an indication of where the ship is. ▼

Astro navigation

Astro means to do with the stars. By the 1400s, sailors were using special instruments, like the astrolabe, to navigate. These instruments measured the angle of the Sun, Moon and particular stars above the horizon. These angles enabled them to work out where they were.

Early instruments were inaccurate. Even today ship's captains have to know how to use old methods, but their instruments are much better. They can tell where a ship is within about 0.6 mile. In the picture on page 23, a crew member is taking a reading of the Sun from the deck of the tanker.

◀ The radar room in a coastline station controls shipping. The operators can send radio messages to ships (that appear as dots on his screen) to prevent collisions.

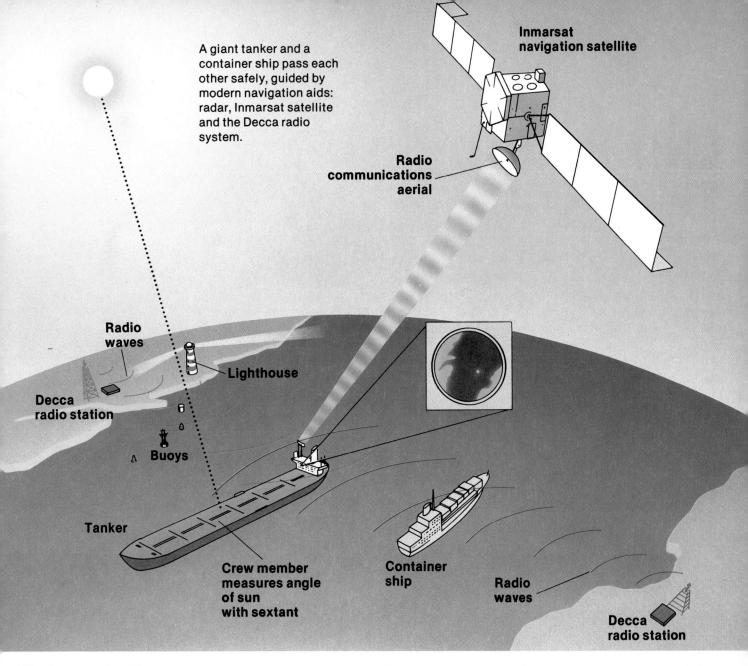

A giant tanker and a container ship pass each other safely, guided by modern navigation aids: radar, Inmarsat satellite and the Decca radio system.

Inmarsat navigation satellite

Radio communications aerial

Radio waves

Lighthouse

Decca radio station

Buoys

Tanker

Crew member measures angle of sun with sextant

Container ship

Radio waves

Decca radio station

Modern navigation

In the past, as well as today, it helped if you could see land. Then you could work out your position by measuring the angles of places on the coast, and it was even better after lighthouses were built.

At the beginning of this century, radio was invented. Soon a way was found to measure the direction of radio stations. This meant that a ship could be up to 50 miles away from the nearest land and still measure the direction of the radio station by picking up radio signals on its receiver. By measuring the directions of two or more stations, the exact position of the ship could be worked out.

Today, special satellites, like the Inmarsats, link over 3,500 ocean-going ships which have 'ship Earth stations' looking like big white thimbles. Each ship station has a computer keyboard, printer, and computer picture screen to help a ship know exactly where it is, and enable the course to be plotted accurately.

Radar

In the past 40 years radar has been fitted to most ships. By sending out radio waves a radar can produce a picture of its surroundings, even in thick fog. It shows other ships nearby. The latest radars can even study the other ships' speed and direction and sound an alarm if a collision is likely.

SHIPS THROUGH THE AGES

This shows how a ship was built in the 1700s.

Foremast

Bowsprit

Outer planking

The first boats were tree-trunks. Later, people used fire and sharp stones to hollow out the trunks and make dug-out canoes. Thousands of years later boat-builders had better tools, such as metal saws and drills. This enabled them to cut smooth planks and fix them together to make bigger ships that were able to sail across the wide oceans.

More than 100 years ago ships were being made of steel. The starting-point was a strong piece like a backbone, called the keel. Then giant curved beams called bulkheads would be added on each side from bow to stern. Then cross-pieces would be added to support the decks. Then thousands of plates would be fixed on the outside to make the hull watertight. Everything would be joined by rivets.

Today giant ships are made in sections inside huge factories. The joints are mostly not riveted but welded. A hot flame is used to heat the edges being joined and melt extra metal from a rod which runs into the joint. When two pieces have been welded they become a single piece of metal. Often the upper parts of a ship are made of aluminum, because of its lightness. When each section is finished it is picked up by a huge crane, placed in position, and welded on.

Today, gigantic tankers are built by welding together 'prefabricated' sections. ▼

These men are building a dug-out canoe about 10,000 years ago. The tree-trunk was hollowed out by burning and chopping with flint axes. Even today, dug-out canoes are still made. ▼

24

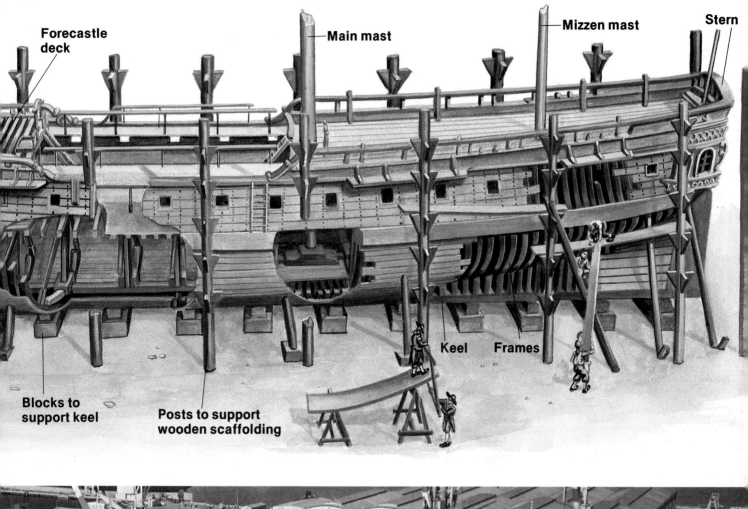

Forecastle deck

Main mast

Mizzen mast

Stern

Keel

Frames

Blocks to support keel

Posts to support wooden scaffolding

The First Boats

How do we know what early boats were like? There are a few ways that we know. The people who built them drew pictures on cave walls or in burial chambers or on pottery, and these pictures have lasted through the ages. One or two early ships have been preserved so well underwater, or in the earth, that we have been able to dig them out. And in many places people still make small boats very much like those of the thousands of years ago.

The earliest boats

As we have said, the first 'boats' were logs that floated on water. Logs were tied together to form rafts. Over the years people discovered how to hollow out logs to make dug-out canoes. Then animal skins were stretched over wooden frames to form boats like coracles. Finally, during the Neolithic period (10,000-3000 BC), people started to make boats from planks of wood fixed together.

The Eastern Mediterranean

The Egyptian civilization centered around the River Nile. Boats played an important part in the life of the Egyptians. In 1850 BC they dug a canal so that boats could sail from the River Nile to the Red Sea. The earliest Egytian boats were made of bundles of papyrus reed. The first known picture of a sailing ship is on a 5,000 year-old Egyptian vase. Trade and wars between the Minoans, Egyptians, Phoenicians, Greeks, Carthaginians and Romans in the Eastern Mediterranean led to rapid improvements in ship design.

This a copy of a carving on the walls of the Borododur Temple in Java. It dates back to AD 500. The canoe, *Sarimanok*, was built using a similar design and materials (palm fibre and bamboo). ►

▲ This picture is based on a model buried in the tomb of an Egyptian about 4,000 years ago. It shows two rafts made by tying together large bundles of papyrus reeds.

▲ Today reed boats are still made in many countries. This one belongs to a fisherman on Lake Titicaca in Peru. The only difference from the old design is that the ends are not curved upwards.

Nordic ships

The earliest known drawings of boats are rock carvings found near Stone Age coastal settlements in Norway. Nordic people (called Vikings), who lived in what is today Denmark, Norway and Sweden, were great explorers. They often buried a dead chief with his ship. The oldest of these ships we have found so far (in 1921) was built about 2,200 years ago. It is 36 feet long and is made of planks of limewood sewn together by a kind of rope.

Simple boats in use today

All over the world people have made small boats for thousands of years. Some of them still use the same methods. In the Far East, Malaysian fishermen sail the same kind of bamboo rafts as their ancestors used. Many boats are still made of watertight animal skins stretched over a light frame. In parts of Wales and Ireland they use this method to make coracles, which are oval boats light enough to be carried on the user's back. For centuries the Inuit of the Arctic have made boats called kayaks, which are long covered canoes with a small hole in the middle for the user.

Many of today's adventurers, like Thor Heyerdahl and Tim Severin, have built boats based on ancient designs. They have used the same building materials and techniques of their predecessors hundreds of years previously. They have made dangerous and adventurous voyages which have proved the seaworthiness of these ancient boats.

◄ To prove that Madagascar could have been populated by the Indonesians 2,500 years ago, Bob Hobman and his crew sailed the *Sarimanok* 4,075 miles from Bali, Indonesia, to Madagascar.

Sailing Ships

Until about 100 years ago almost every ocean-going ship had sails. Even if a ship had an engine it kept sails as well, because in those days engines often broke down. More than one thousand different kinds of sailing ship have been made and over 200 types are still in use.

Life on board

Life on a sailing ship — whether it was a sixteenth century Spanish galleon or a nineteenth century Clipper like the *Cutty Sark* — was hard work. Lots of sailors were needed to do the work. Depending on the weather, the huge sails had to be let down to catch the wind, or furled (rolled up) against their yards. Big sails could weigh a ton or more, and the whole ship was a mass of ropes, called sheets, which formed the 'rigging' needed to control the sails. The ropes were often thick and heavy.

Ropes and sails always needed repair. The crew had to be experts in tying knots.

▲ This big sailing ship is often called a 'Tall Ship.' Some are used to give teenagers experience of working together under what are sometimes difficult conditions on the sea.

Sailors had to bind the ends of ropes and stitch sails using huge needles (knocked by mallets through the thick canvas) and heavy waxed thread. Sometimes a picture or badge would be painted on the sail. Near the top of the mast would be fixed a small platform, called the crow's nest, where men would stand on permanent look-out duty.

Making life easier

Over 200 years ago new inventions made life easier. The pulley block enabled one man to pull a rope as hard as six or even ten men.

▲ This is part of the famous Bayeux Tapestry which records the Norman conquest of England in 1066. It shows the Norman fleet setting out.

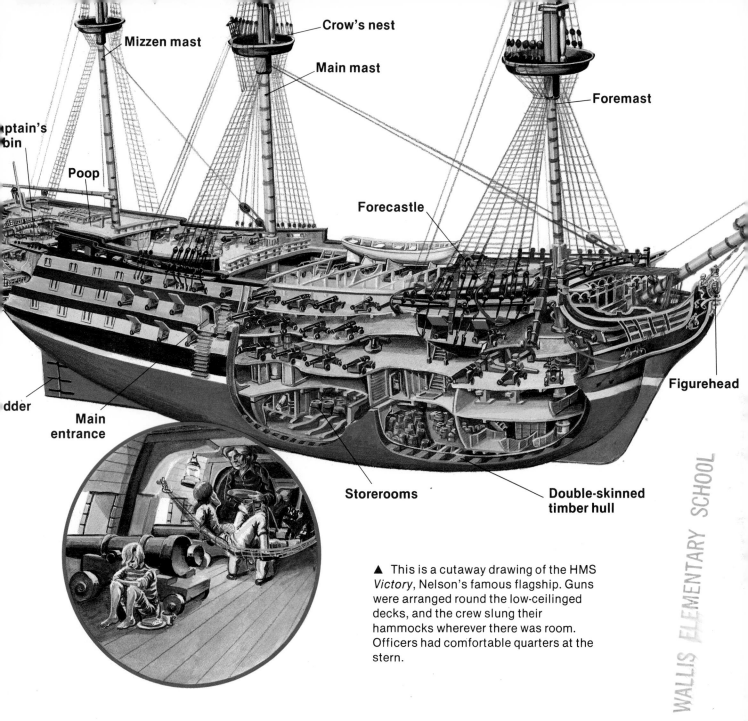

Mizzen mast

Crow's nest

Main mast

Foremast

Captain's cabin

Poop

Forecastle

Rudder

Main entrance

Figurehead

Storerooms

Double-skinned timber hull

▲ This is a cutaway drawing of the HMS *Victory*, Nelson's famous flagship. Guns were arranged round the low-ceilinged decks, and the crew slung their hammocks wherever there was room. Officers had comfortable quarters at the stern.

The capstan was a vertical drum with spokes; many men could push on the spokes and wind a rope on the drum with a force of several tons. New fabrics made sails lighter, and stronger. Heavy ropes made from vegetable fibers were replaced by thin steel cables. By the late 1800s big sailing ships could be managed by quite a small crew, and this made it possible to give each man better conditions. Sailors used to tie a hammock, a bed made from a single piece of sailcloth, in the same crowded space as 20 or 30 of their mates, but after 1900 they began to have beds!

Modern ocean yachts

Old sailing ships had masts and spars of wood, but today's yacht uses aluminum or carbon fiber. Brass, bronze or painted steel fittings have been replaced by stainless steel and strong plastics, which need no paint. Wooden or painted steel hulls have been replaced by fiberglass and foam sandwich which is light and rigid and cannot rust or rot. Sails are of nylon and similar weather-proof but lightweight fabric, and so are the ropes. Modern rachet handles with gearboxes enable one person to manage a huge sail.

Age of Steam

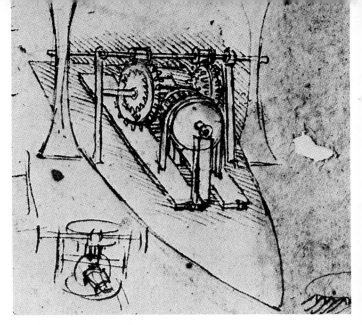

When steam engines were proposed as a means of propelling ships more than 200 years ago, most people said they could never work. In fact the steam engine and the boat went together perfectly.

Although most early steamships had sails as well as steam engines, the one great advantage of having an engine was that you could go where you wanted no matter which way the wind was blowing.

The first steamships

The idea of powering ships using steam engines was first suggested in the middle of the 1700s. By 1830 the first paddle steamers were in use in France, Britain and America. One of the first steamships to cross the Atlantic was the *Great Britain*. The *Great Britain* was

▲ This is a sketch made by Leonardo da Vinci, an inventor and artist, about 500 years ago. It shows how an engine could drive two paddle wheels to propel a ship.

designed by the British engineer, Isambard Kingdom Brunel. When it was launched in Bristol in 1843 it was the largest ship in the world. It was the first large ocean-going ship to be made entirely of iron, as well as the first screw-fitted steamer to cross the Atlantic. The steam engines in most early steamboats powered paddles on each side of the ship, as you can see in the drawing of another of Brunel's ships, the *Great Eastern*, on page 17.

The first turbine ship, *Turbinia*, is dwarfed by the turbine-engined liner *Mauretania*.

▲ The launch of Brunel's *Great Britain,* at Bristol in 1843. It was the first transatlantic liner with a screw instead of paddle wheels.

The *Delta Queen* paddle boat steams up the Mississippi River. It was built in 1926. Mississippi paddle boats have paddle wheels at the stern. ▼

The great liners

The world's greatest liners were the ones built to carry passengers and mail across the Atlantic. The Blue Riband was a prize awarded for the fastest Atlantic crossing. Many nations competed for this prize. The British liner, the *Mauretania,* held the prize for the longest time. The *Mauretania* was put into service in 1907. The secret of its success was that it had steam turbine engines which almost doubled its power. The turbines drove four propellers, and needed 25 boilers to supply the steam.

Deep down in the hot boiler rooms of these liners, an army of sweating stokers spent their working lives shovelling coal into the fires under the boilers. Imagine doing that all day, with the ship rolling in a storm. Other holders of the Blue Riband were the French liner *Normandie* and the last holder of the prize, the American liner the *United States.*

The age of the great Atlantic passenger ships, called 'liners' lasted from 1900 to 1960. First-class passengers had fantastic luxury, as good as the best hotels and restaurants on land. But by 1957 more people flew the Atlantic than travelled by sea. Today there are only a few big passenger liners, like the *Queen Elizabeth 2,* which carry people on holiday cruises.

Modern Ships

Today, there are more different kinds of ships than ever. Most of them do the same tasks as they have done down the centuries: ferrying people and cargo, defense and fishing. But there are unusual ships today which would have surprised our ancestors.

Cargo ships

Cargo ships can carry containers, or 'bulk cargo' such as grain. Containers are large boxes filled at a factory and lifted straight on to a ship by crane. If cargo ships carry meat or fruit they are made like giant floating refrigerators. LNG (liquefied natural gas) carriers carry a row of enormous spheres, each holding thousands of tons of freezing liquid. The biggest ships of all are oil tankers. The biggest tanker in the world is the *Seawise Giant*. It is 1,250 feet long and weighs more than half a million tons.

Ferries

Ferries are ships that carry people between ports that are not far apart. Some are called Ro-Ro (roll on, roll off) ferries because cars, buses and trucks can drive on board and drive off. Often the whole bow of the ship hinges up like a giant door. A few ferries have railway tracks and carry trains.

Warships

Today, most warships are much smaller than the huge battleships built in the early 1900s. They are called frigates, destroyers or patrol boats. Much of the running of the ship is computer-controlled, so the crew are a small, highly skilled team. By far the biggest modern warships are the giant aircraft carriers. These are like floating cities, carrying more than 6000 people. On top is the flight deck, from where as many as 90 aircraft can go into action.

The *Queen Elizabeth 2,* or *'QE2'*, is the biggest passenger ship still in use. It is much smaller than the biggest liners of 50 years ago. ▼

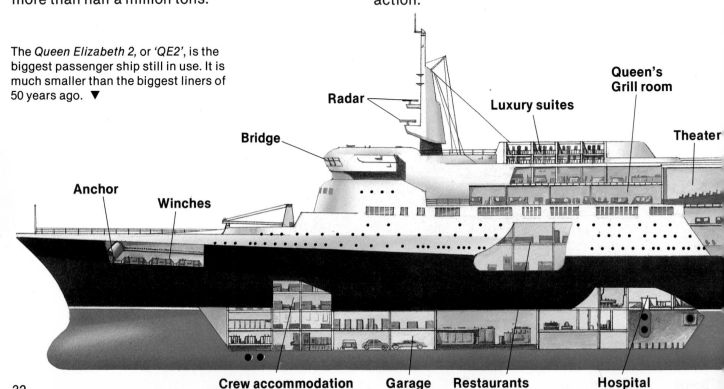

Radar · Bridge · Luxury suites · Queen's Grill room · Theater · Anchor · Winches · Crew accommodation · Garage · Restaurants · Hospital

The nuclear-powered icebreaker, the *Arktika*, keeps the Arctic sea lanes open.

Working ships

Some ships never go very far but have to be ready for action at a moment's notice. An example is the fire float. When a fire breaks out near a river, the fire float rushes there and pumps water and foam at the fire. Dredgers usually stay in the same port or river and spend their lives digging out the muddy bottom to keep the water deep enough for bigger ships. Lightships never go anywhere! They stay anchored on one spot, carrying a lighthouse to guide other ships. Icebreakers, like the 25,000 ton *Lenin*, have very strong hulls. They are needed in places like Canada and the Soviet Union to keep rivers and harbors open in winter.

Britain's aircraft carrier, HMS *Illustrious,* carries helicopters and Sea Harrier jump jets. ▶

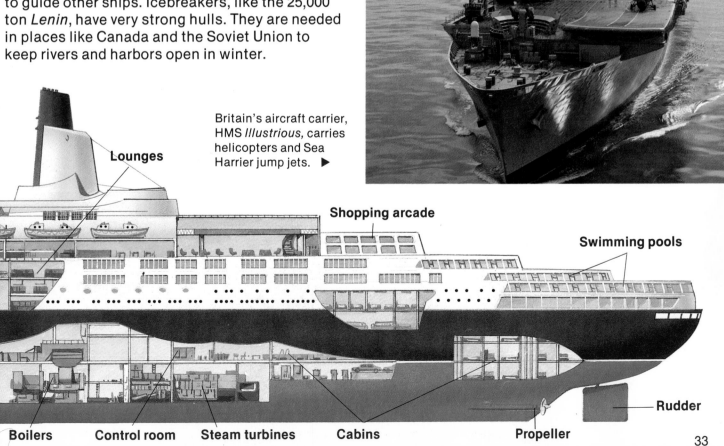

Lounges

Shopping arcade

Swimming pools

Rudder

Boilers   **Control room**   **Steam turbines**   **Cabins**   **Propeller**

FUN AND FEAR ON WATER

Hundreds of years ago almost everyone was afraid of the sea. Hardly anyone could swim. Travelling by ship was very dangerous. Hundreds of ships were wrecked every year. Most just disappeared; nobody every knew what happened to them. Some thought that they had sailed over the edge of the Earth, or been devoured by gigantic sea monsters.

But even today, with strong, stable ships, good communications and efficient rescue services, the sea must be treated with great respect. Even the biggest ships are at the mercy of the weather. Storms and hurricanes can blow up from nowhere. They whip up mountainous seas that threaten to engulf any ships that dare to leave the safety of a port. Ships also risk running aground on to jagged rocks, colliding with other ships in the crowded waterways of the world, or hitting icebergs. In 1986 the support ship to the British expedition to the South Pole was crushed by ice, and sank.

But today, disasters at sea are rare. Every day all over the world, millions of people of all ages have fun on rivers, lakes and on the sea. There is one basic rule if you want to keep safe: always be sure to know what you are doing, and do it correctly. And if you are going out far from land, always wear a lifejacket.

◀ Fun on water ought to be possible without fear. These children are racing dinghies in Devon, England, on a bright summer's day.

What a contrast is this picture of the treacherous North Sea in winter! The ship services oil rigs (the one in the background is the Ekofisk field where a large rig collapsed in a gale). It is tossed about like a cork by the stormy sea.

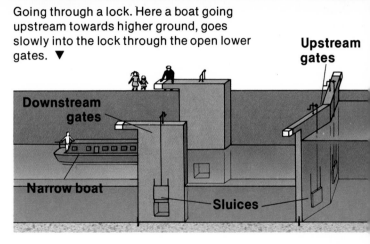
Going through a lock. Here a boat going upstream towards higher ground, goes slowly into the lock through the open lower gates. ▼

Upstream gates

Downstream gates

Narrow boat

Sluices

Inland Water Travel

We have already seen that the first boats were used on rivers, and this is an example of inland water travel. One of the world's greatest 'highways' is the River Rhine. Every day over a million tons of cargo travels along it. It joins Switzerland to the North Sea, flowing between Germany, France and through Holland. Nearly all the traffic consists of huge barges. A barge is a boat specially designed for inland load-carrying. Most are rather narrow, and they have shallow draught, which means that the bottom does not go very deep down into the water.

Canals

Many rivers are useful as inland waterways, though a few rush over weirs, rocky rapids or even waterfalls, which means they cannot be used. But about 200 years ago the roads were so bad that people decided to build artificial rivers, or canals. Some canals, like the Panama Canal in Central America, join two seas or oceans, to make a journey much shorter.

It takes a lot of digging to make a canal. When the land goes up or down, the canal needs locks. A lock is a short section of canal which can be shut off at both ends with tight-fitting gates. Look at the diagram above to see how locks work. It is quite hard work opening and closing the canal gates, and the various sluices, but it is the only way to make boats go up and down hills!

The gaily painted 'narrow boats' of the English canals were built to carry heavy goods. Today they carry people on holiday.

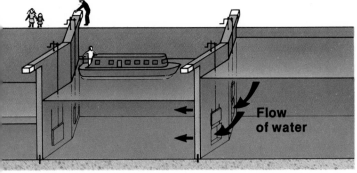

With both sets of gates tightly closed, the water inside the lock is brought up to the higher level by opening the sluices (small doors) in the upper gates. ▼

Flow of water

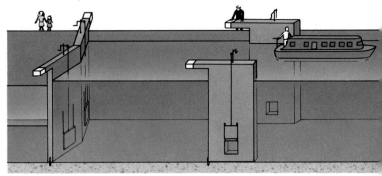

When the water reaches the higher level the upstream gates can be opened and the boat goes on its way. First, the crew must close the open sluices. ▼

Britain's engineers dug many canals between 1750-1850. At first they made a great difference to inland transport, carrying tons of goods throughout the country. A horse could only pull a one-ton load along muddy roads, but it could pull 50 tons in a canal barge. By 1945 the canals were falling into disuse. They were blocked with mud, and goods travelled by rail, road and air instead.

Today many of the canals have been restored, but only for fun. Thousands of people each year hire a 'narrow boat' — many of which are real old canal barges — so that their family can spend their holiday travelling at walking pace up a peaceful old canal.

Water buses

A water bus is like any other city bus but it goes on water. Many cities have rivers or canals running through them. Tourists use water buses mainly for fun, but in some cities they are used by the locals as a really good way to get about.

The city of Venice in Italy has no roads at all. If you open your front door, there beyond the doorstep is cold, dark water! The only way to get about is by boat. Most of the boats are called gondolas. They are water taxis. You get in and tell the gondolier where you want to go. He paddles you there with great skill. Gondolas carry two or three people, mostly tourists.

▲ Sometimes water travel is the only form of travel possible. This boat is on a river deep in the South American rain-forest.

Racing on Water

Everyone likes to watch a race, and most of us like to take part. Over the years, people have used water for every possible kind of race.

Racing with oars

Special rowing boats are designed for racing. They are called by such names as skiffs or shells. They are extremely long, and pointed at each end, but only just wide enough for someone to sit on. The oars are pivoted a long way out from the sides of the boat, on a strong but light triangle.

Canoe races

One type of canoe race is called a slalom. On a fast-moving river, competitors have to weave in and out along a row of poles or gateways, without hitting any of the uprights. Even trickier are 'white water' races. Canoeists have to paddle through the rapids without hitting the rocks and capsizing.

Power boats

This is the name given to speedboats with engines. Some are small, and race on rivers and reservoirs. The biggest race across the sea, even from America to England!

There are lots of classes. By far the most numerous classes are called outboards, which have the engine and propeller fixed on the back outside the boat. Inboards have bigger engines, and the fastest of all have aircraft-type jet engines. Today the highest speed reached with a water propeller is 202 MPH, and the highest speed with a jet engine is just over 316 MPH. At such speeds hitting the water is like hitting a brick wall. Many people who tried to break speed records on water have been killed, such as Donald Campbell in 1967.

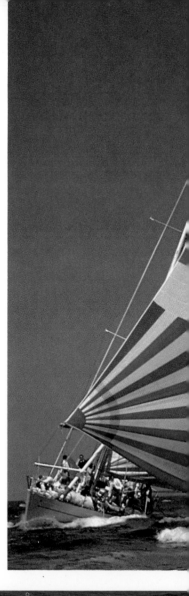

These yachts are racing on Lake Ontario, Canada. Their billowing front sails are called spinnakers. Each yacht keels over in the stiff breeze. ▶

Power boat racing is very exciting. Giant boats with engines of 1,000 horsepower or more, and usually with a small two-seat cockpit, thunder across the waves at the speed of a fast car. ▼

This canoe is a competitor in a white-water 'slalom' event. The canoe has to go between pairs of poles without the canoe or paddle touching either. ▼

Racing with sails

There are about 905 different classes of racing boats with sails! Some of the classes are big: there are almost 2,000,000 center-board dinghies. Big ocean-going yachts cost millions of dollars, so there are only a few of these. They need a big crew to manage them, whereas the smallest boats are 'single-handed', which means there is only one person on board. The smallest class of all, the Optimist, is popular with children.

Some of the fastest sailing boats are called multihulls. If they have two hulls, fixed wide apart side-by-side, they are called catamarans. If they have a central hull with a smaller hull on each side they are called trimarans. If they have a main hull joined to a small float on one side only they are called proas. The fastest sailing boat ever built is a proa.

Disaster and Rescue

Although we use the word disaster to mean an event that kills many people, we must remember that a single death is disastrous to the family concerned. There used to be many disasters and shipwrecks, but today they are rare, and rescue services are much improved.

Famous disasters

The most famous sea disaster of all was the sinking of the *Titanic*. The *Titanic* was the biggest and fastest passenger ship in the world. During its first trip from Southampton to New York at nearly midnight on April 14, 1912 the passengers felt a slight bump. They thought nothing had happened and carried on eating, dancing and enjoying themselves. When it was discovered that the ship had hit an iceberg, ripping the hull open, still nobody believed the *Titanic* would sink. They were wrong. The 'unsinkable' *Titanic* sank and about 1500 people were drowned.

The worst sea disaster of all time happened at the end of World War Two, in 1945. A Russian submarine torpedoed a passenger ship, the *Wilhelm Gustloff,* that was overcrowded with refugees. About 7,700 people died.

Oil spills

Giant tankers now carry as much as half a million tons of thick black oil. If the oil were to leak out it would pollute a vast area of sea and coastline, and kill millions of fish and birds. The first such disaster was on March 18, 1967 when the *Torrey Canyon* ran on to rocks off Cornwall and broke in two.

One of the latest ways to rescue people at sea is by helicopter. Here, a Wessex resuce helicopter of the British RAF practices winching a 'survivor' to safety. ▶

▲ In 1912, the *Titanic* hit an iceberg and sank.

Safety on board

Every large ship must be equipped with things intended to prevent danger and save life. There must be equipment for fighting fires, plenty of lifejackets and lifebelts and lifeboats to enable everyone on board to get away if the ship should sink. The lifeboats should be equipped with emergency drinking water, radio and medical supplies. Until the 1930s a ship's lifeboats were rowed, but modern ones have engines. They are self-righting; if a wave knocks one over, it turns right way up again.

Rescue services

Before World War Two, the only kind of sea rescue service was provided by lifeboats. These were kept around the coasts of most countries. Many people have risked their lives to rescue people in danger on the sea. Lifeboats of Britain's Royal National Lifeboat Institution (RNLI), started in 1854, have made many daring rescues. The worst tragedy of the RNLI's history was in 1886 when 27 lifeboatmen drowned while trying to rescue the crew of a ship that had gone aground off the Lancashire coast.

Since World War Two, most countries with a coastline have airplanes and helicopters standing by day and night, ready to go and rescue people. Helicopters are fitted with winches which can pull people straight up out of the sea or off the deck of a sinking ship.

One of the biggest disasters of recent years was the wreck of the giant tanker *Amoco Cadiz* in 1978. Here the sea is breaking over its superstructure. ▼

Books and Places

Books to read

Wooden Ship (Adkins, Jan) Houghton-Mifflin, 1978

Submarines (Humble, Richard) F. Watts, 1985

Clipper ships and Captains (Lyon, Jane D.) American Heritage, 1962

Ships (Rutland, Jonathan) Warwick, 1982

"The Seafarers" (20 volumes) Time-Life Books

Supertanker! The Story of the World's Biggest Ships (Sullivan, George) Dodd Mead 1978

Oars, Sails and Steam; A Picture Book of Ships (Tunis, Edwin) Crowell, 1977

Surface Warships (VanTol, Robert) F. Watts, 1985

H. W. Wilson's Standard Catalog latest edition

Places to visit

National Maritime Museum, San Francisco, California; United States Naval Academy Museum, Annapolis, Maryland; San Diego Maritime Museum, San Diego, California; South Street Seaport Museum, New York, New York; Philadelphia Maritime Museum, Philadelphia, Pennsylvania; Intrepid Sea-Air-Space Museum, New York, New York

Golden Hind (98 ft. long)

Dates

30,000 BC? There is no way of knowing when the first small boat was made, but it might have been as long ago as this.

3000 BC by this time big boats were being made in Egypt. They were made of planks and had sails and a crew of 30 men.

AD 98? Eric the Red set out from Iceland and is believed to have reached what is now the USA.

AD 600 By this time Arab ships were using the lateen (triangular) sail which could sail almost against the wind.

1100 About this time British ships appeared with hinged rudders.

1519-1522 An expedition, led at the start by Magellan, sails around the world for the first time.

This is a scale drawing of the world's biggest supertanker, the *Seawise Giant;* the battleship HMS *Deadnought;* the *Golden Hind;* and a modern passenger ferry.

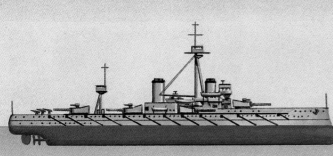

Seawise Giant (1,250 ft. long)

HMS *Dreadnought* (436 ft. long)

Modern ferry (286 ft. long)

Biggest and Fastest

1736 Jonathan Hull in England built a paddleboat driven by an early steam engine.
1894 The first turbine-engined boat, the *Turbinia,* is built.
1898 John Holland in the USA builds the first practical submarine.
1904 The first steam-turbine passenger liner, followed in
1906 by the turbine-engined battleship *Dreadnought.*
1912 The first diesel-engined ship, the Danish *Selandia.*
1941 Biggest passenger ship of all time, *Queen Elizabeth.*
1952 Fastest passenger ship, *United States.*
1954 Submarine *Nautilus,* first ship driven by nuclear energy.
1959 The first hovercraft, Britain's *SR.N1.*

Biggest passenger ship
Britain's *Queen Elizabeth,* 83,673 tons, but the *France* (later renamed *Norway*) was slightly longer, though only 66,384 tons

Biggest battleship
Japan's *Yamato* and *Musashi,* each of 72,809 tons. Both were completed and then sunk in World War Two.

Biggest warships
US Navy aircraft carriers *Nimitz, Dwight D. Eisenhower* and *Carl Vinson,* each of 91,400 tons. Their flight decks are 1,090 ft. long and 252 ft wide.
Other US carriers are almost as big.

Biggest oil tanker
Seawise Giant, 564,733 tons, was built in Japan but flies the Liberian flag. It is 1,504 ft long.

Fastest passenger ship
SS *United States,* which on its maiden voyage in 1952 crossed the Atlantic at a speed of 35.59 knots (41 mph).

Fastest warship
French destroyer *Le Terrible* of 1935, which reached 45.25 knots (52.1 mph).

Fastest submarine
Either the US *Los Angeles* class or the Soviet *Alpha* class, both of which are believed to exceed 42 knots (48.5 mph) when submerged.

Fastest hovercraft
US Navy's SES (surface effect ship) 100B which in 1980 reached 91.9 knots (105.8 mph).

Fastest practical sailing boat
Special catamaran *Beowulf V,* timed in 1974 at 36.16 mph.

Fastest boat
Spirit of Australia jet propelled speedboat, which in 1978 reached 319.6 mph.

Fastest rowing boat
Oxford 'racing eight' which won the boat race in 1984 against Cambridge in the record time of 16 minutes 45 seconds, an average speed of 15.09 mph.

WALLIS ELEMENTARY SCHOOL

Word List

Battleship A big ship carrying the largest guns and protected by thick armor. The last were made 40 year ago.

Blue Riband The honor given to the liner which made the fastest crossing of the Atlantic.

Bow The front of a ship. Often an s is put on the end (someone might be "standing in the bows"), though each ship has only one bow.

Buoy A kind of floating signpost or warning sign anchored near ports and harbors.

Canoe A simple small boat driven along by a paddle.

Capsize To roll right over.

Clippers Fast sailing ships used in the 1800s to transport goods and passengers over long distances.

Compass An instrument with a dial and pointer connected to a magnet to show which direction is North.

Coracle A small boat used in Wales and Ireland. It is made of skins stretched on a light, wooden frame.

Cox A person who steers a racing rowing boat.

Decks The floors of a ship.

Dinghy Various kinds of small boats, some with sails and others (including inflatable rubber ones) with paddles.

Displacement The weight of water displaced by a ship. This is the same as the actual weight of the ship and everything in it.

Galleon A large sailing ship of 300 to 500 years ago, much higher at the ends than in the middle.

Galley A long, low and narrow ship of from 400 to more than 3,000 years ago, with sails and dozens of oars.

Hovercraft A vessel that hovers on a cushion of air.

Hull The main body of a ship.

Inflatable Blown up with air, or gas.

Keel The lowest part of a ship, often made specially heavy to keep the ship the right way up. Yachts have deep flat-sided keels to stop the sails pushing the whole boat sideways.

Knot A speed of one nautical mile per hour. A nautical mile is 6,080 feet, so a knot is 8 mph.

Lifeboat A small but specially designed boat which can go out in the worst storms to rescue people at sea.

Mast The tall pole on which sails are fastened.

Port A seaside place where ships load and unload cargoes. The same word also means the left side of a ship.

Raft A simple boat with no keel, and usually no engine, often made of logs tied together.

Rigging All the ropes and wires needed to support masts and sails.

Rudder The hinged plate at the stern used for steering a ship.

Satellite An automatic spacecraft that orbits the Earth.

Starboard The right side of a ship, or the right-hand direction.

Stern The back of a ship.

Tacking Sailing on a zig-zag course.

Yacht Most yachts are fast sailing boats used for racing, but the word is also used for big luxury boats, with engines, used for pleasure.

Index